Thinking Through Science
Activities from Chemistry 1

Stephen Beer   David Edwards   Roland Jackson

SERIES EDITOR: DAVID EDWARDS

UNWIN HYMAN

Published in 1989 by
Unwin Hyman Limited
15-17 Broadwick Street
London W1V 1FP

© Stephen Beer, David Edwards, Roland Jackson 1989

All rights reserved. No part of this publication may be reproduced, stored in a retrieval system, or transmitted in any form or by any means, electronic mechanical, photocopying, recording or otherwise, without the prior permission of Unwin Hyman Limited.

British Library Cataloguing in Publication Data

Edwards, David, *1950*–
   Activities from chemistry.—(Thinking through science).
   Bk. 1
   1. Chemistry. Experiments
   I. Title II. Beer, Stephen III. Jackson, Roland, *1954*–
   IV. Series
   542

ISBN 0-7135-2850-8

Typeset by MS Filmsetting Ltd, Frome
Origination by Chroma Graphics, Singapore
Printed and bound by New Interlitho, Italy

Cover photograph by Martyn Chillmaid
Book design by Juliet and Charles Snape

Contents

About this book (v)

Unit
1. Gold — 2
2. Oil — 4
3. Kitchen Cleaners — 6
4. Acids — 8
5. Corrosion Testing — 10
6. Accident! — 12
7. Swap Shop — 14
8. Now you see it... Now you don't — 16
9. The Water Cycle — 18
10. Acid Drops — 20
11. Fire! — 22
12. Getting Bread to Rise — 24
13. Salt of the Earth — 26
14. Alcool — 28
15. Camping Gas — 30
16. Fizzy Drinks — 32
17. Feed the World — 34
18. Which Oil? — 36
19. Healthy Eating — 38
20. Extracting Zinc — 40

Content Matrix for the National Curriculum — 42
Index — 43
Acknowledgements — 44

About this book

These exercises are about important applications of chemistry. Some of the information you will have to read – some of it you will have to get from the tables, charts and pictures. You will use this information and what you already know about chemistry to answer the questions.

Thinking Through Science, Chemistry 1 will help you to understand some useful chemical ideas. But most of all, we hope that the book will let you enjoy chemistry – a very important part of our everyday lives.

1 GOLD

NEW GOLD FIND IN CALIFORNIA!

£MILLIONS STOLEN IN BRINKS-MAT GOLD ROBBERY!

For centuries people have looked for this rare and precious metal. For miners, criminals and ordinary men and women, the attraction is the same. Gold is beautiful and valuable.

Most of the world's gold (about 60%) comes from South Africa, but even there it is rare and difficult to mine. The deepest gold mine, the Western Deep Levels, is 4 km below the surface. A lot of rock has to be dug out to get even a small amount of gold—about 2 tonnes to get enough for a ring! This is why gold is so expensive. A one centimetre cube could cost you £200!

Ever since gold was first discovered, it is likely to have been used as money. Although we don't pay for things in gold coins today, the metal is still an important part of trading between countries.

But gold has other uses too. These depend on the *properties* of gold, which are listed in the Factfile.

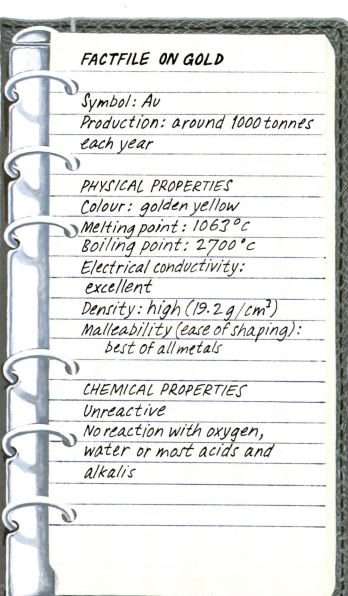

FACTFILE ON GOLD

Symbol: Au
Production: around 1000 tonnes each year

PHYSICAL PROPERTIES
Colour: golden yellow
Melting point: 1063°C
Boiling point: 2700°C
Electrical conductivity: excellent
Density: high (19.2 g/cm^3)
Malleability (ease of shaping): best of all metals

CHEMICAL PROPERTIES
Unreactive
No reaction with oxygen, water or most acids and alkalis

1. Which properties of gold are typical of a metal?

2. What would happen to a gold bar if you heated it to 1100°C?

3. Why is gold found "native" (on its own as an element)?

4. Which property of gold is important in "panning"? (In this process, the gold is separated by swirling fine gold-bearing material in a pan of water. The gold stays in the middle of the pan.)

specks of gold — grit etc.

5. Which country produces most of the world's gold?

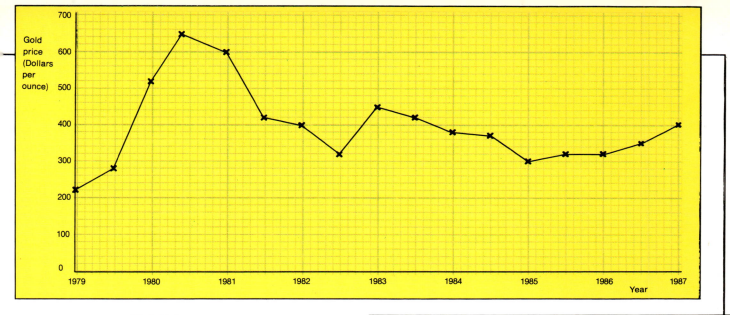

Rich Pickens (banker)
I use gold for investment.

Carlo da Munni (coin dealer)
I deal in gold medals and coins.

Julie Case (jeweller)
I use gold to make jewellery.

Ivor Littlebit (electronic engineer)
I use gold in electrical circuits.

Art Gilder (artist)
I use gold to decorate.

Phyllis Cavity (dentist)
I use gold in fillings.

6. What was the price of gold at the beginning of 1982?

7. During which year was gold most expensive?

8. Imagine you bought 10 ounces of gold at the start of 1981 and sold them at the start of 1987. How much money would you have made or lost?

9. What do you think would happen to the price of gold during a long strike by South African miners?

10. Which properties of gold make it useful for each of the following people?

(a) Jeweller   (d) Banker

(b) Electronics engineer   (e) Coin dealer

(c) Dentist   (f) Artist

11. Between 1979 and 1980 the gold price rose rapidly. During this time, which of the six people opposite would you *most* have liked to be? Which would you have *least* liked to be? Give your reasons.

2 OIL

Using oil

Crude oil is mixture of many different *hydro-carbons*—chemicals which contain only hydrogen and carbon atoms.

Crude oil is not much use until it is separated into more useful parts, called *fractions*. This is done by fractional distillation.

Most of the fractions are burnt as fuels. The rest go to make plastics, detergents and many other important chemicals.

1. What is a hydrocarbon?

2. Octane is a hydrocarbon which has eight carbon atoms. Which fraction would you find it in?

3. Which property of hydrocarbons is used to separate them?

4. Which fraction has the lowest boiling range?

5. Which fraction would be the hardest to boil?

6. Which of the fractions are burnt as fuels?

7. Which fraction do you think there is most demand for in the world?

8. What do you think would happen to the price of crude oil if:

    (a) all countries banned the use of nuclear power?

    (b) the Persian Gulf, through which most of the West's oil is carried, was closed by war?

THE FRACTIONS

GASES

1–4 carbon atoms
Boiling range:
up to 40°C
For heating/cooking

PETROL/NAPHTHA

4–12 carbon atoms
Boiling range:
30°C–65°C (petrol)
65°C–300°C (naphtha)
Petrol for cars
For making plastics

KEROSENE

9–16 carbon atoms
Boiling range:
150°C–240°C
Fuel for jets
Heating oil for houses

DIESEL OIL

15–25 carbon atoms
Boiling range:
220°C–250°C
Fuel for diesel
engines and tractors

LUBRICATING OIL

20+ carbon atoms
Boiling range:
250°C–350°C
Engine oil

BITUMEN

Many carbon atoms
Boiling range:
over 350°C
For roads, roofing

When the oil runs out

Crude oil is a *finite resource*. That means that there is only a limited amount in the earth. Eventually it will be used up. Read what people have said about this:

- Some geologists say we've only got about 40 years' supply left
- We're running out of North Sea Oil already
- Oil will become very expensive, so people will buy other fuels
- We'll use alternative energy sources, like wind and solar power
- I'm worried about radioactive pollution from nuclear power stations
- We can make fuels and chemicals from coal—we used to before we found oil
- We'll find new supplies of oil
- There'll be wars as people fight for the oil that's left
- We'll use nuclear energy
- I think we should save energy
- People are too sensible to fight over oil
- As the oil runs out, *all* fuels will become more expensive
- If alternative energies are so good, why don't we use them now?
- Coal will run out faster

9. Decide what *you* think might happen if the oil runs out.
10. Write a paragraph of 100–150 words explaining what you think will happen.

3 KITCHEN CLEANERS

Kitchen cleaners are some of the most useful household chemicals. But they can be dangerous.

The makers of kitchen cleaners take a lot of trouble to tell us about the dangers. The labels they use are eye-catching. But how often do we bother to read their warnings?

Now here's your big chance!

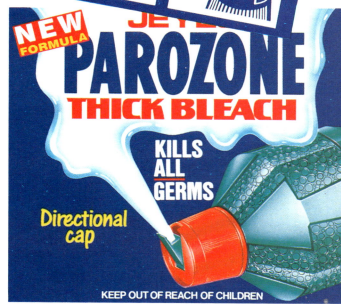

1. Why have the makers of this bleach designed a bottle top that is difficult to open?

2. What *two* jobs does PAROZONE bleach do?

3. What is the active ingredient in PAROZONE? What gas do you think was used to make this ingredient?

4. What do you think the word "irritant" means?

5. Why is it useful to have the symbol for irritant as well as the word on the label?

6. Why do you think bleach should *not* be mixed with other chemicals?

7. Why should bleach be diluted before it is used on clothes?

8. Why should you not remove the label until the bottle is empty?

9. Your next-door neighbour wants to borrow some bleach. They have brought round a pop bottle. Why should you refuse?

This scouring powder also contains a bleach. It also contains a detergent and an abrasive powder. The abrasive powder is made of limestone rock which has been crushed very finely.

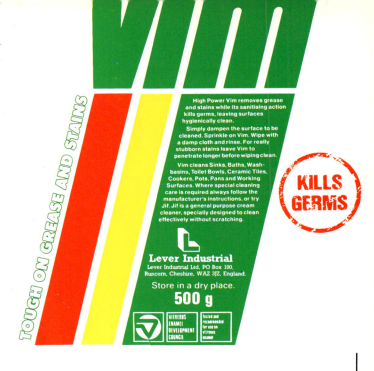

10. What evidence on the label suggests that VIM contains a bleach?

11. Why do you think a detergent is used in VIM?

12. Why do you think VIM contains an abrasive?

13. Suggest why scouring powders which contain abrasives are becoming less popular.

The third kitchen cleaner to look at is called OVEN PAD. As the name suggests, it removes grease and dirt from ovens. Once again, this cleaner contains a harmful chemical – a strong alkali called sodium hydroxide.

The makers have taken a lot of trouble to tell us how to use OVEN PAD safely.

OVEN PAD works because alkalis like sodium hydroxide react chemically with grease. The products of the reaction are soluble in water and can be washed away.

14. Why can't the grease be removed by washing the oven with water?

15. What do you think the pH of sodium hydroxide solution would be? Describe what you would do to find out.

16. What word is used on this label to describe the danger from sodium hydroxide?

17. How should you protect yourself from this danger?

18. What should you do if sodium hydroxide is spilled onto your skin?

19. What information on the label suggests that this reaction is slow?

20. How can this chemical reaction be speeded up?

21. Why do you think that OVEN PAD should not be used on a very hot oven?

4 ACIDS

Acids are very important chemicals. They get involved in a lot of chemical reactions.

When acids are added to most metals, hydrogen gas is formed. Here are three examples.

Zinc and hydrochloric acid react to give hydrogen gas and zinc chloride

Magnesium and nitric acid react to give hydrogen gas and magnesium nitrate

Iron and sulphuric acid react to give hydrogen gas and iron sulphate

In each case, the metal takes the place of the hydrogen in the acid.

A good way of showing what happens is to use a word equation:

zinc	+	hydrochloric acid	→	zinc chloride	+	hydrogen
iron	+	nitric acid	→	iron nitrate	+	hydrogen
magnesium	+	sulphuric acid	→	magnesium sulphate	+	hydrogen

In all of these reactions, the chemicals formed from the metal and part of the acid are called SALTS.

We can now see a pattern.

ACID + METAL → SALT + HYDROGEN

Different acids form different salts.

ACID	NAME OF ITS SALTS
citric acid	citrates
ethanoic acid	ethanoates
hydrochloric acid	chlorides
methanoic acid	methanoates
nitric acid	nitrates
phosphoric acid	phosphates
stearic acid	stearates
sulphuric acid	sulphates
tartaric acid	tartrates

1. What do all the endings of the names of the acids have in common?

2. All but one of the names for the salts have something in common. Why are the names of the salts formed from hydrochloric acid the odd ones out?

3. What do all the other names for salts have in common?

4. Predict the names of the salts which form from

   (a) oxalic acid;
   (b) benzoic acid.

5. Suggest the full names for the salts formed when

   (a) calcium metal reacts with tartaric acid;
   (b) magnesium metal reacts with ethanoic acid;
   (c) iron reacts with hydrochloric acid.

Acids also react with chemicals called bases. Most bases are
- the oxides of metals

OR
- the hydroxides of metals (if these dissolve in water they are also called alkalis)

OR
- carbonates (including hydrogencarbonates)

Some of the reactions between acids and bases are very useful.

Brass ornaments can be cleaned with lemon juice. Citric acid in the lemon reacts with the copper oxide on the surface to form copper citrate and water.

Too much hydrochloric acid in the stomach causes indigestion. The magnesium hydroxide in these tablets reacts with the acid to make magnesium chloride and water.

These fizzy sweets contain citric acid and sodium hydrogencarbonate. When you suck these sweets the chemicals react to form sodium citrate, water and carbon dioxide gas.

6. Write word equations for each of the reactions shown in the pictures.

7. Name the chemical that is formed every time an acid reacts with a base.

8. Name the three salts formed in these reactions.

9. Which product of these reactions is formed only when an acid reacts with a carbonate.

10. Complete these equations to show what happens when acids react with different types of bases.

(a) ACID + METAL OXIDE   → _____ + _____

(b) ACID + ALKALI   → _____ + _____

(c) ACID + CARBONATE   → _____ + _____ + _____

These pictures show some other examples of acids and bases.

11. Predict the products of the reaction when:

(a) the iron oxide in rust is removed by phosphoric acid.

(b) the aluminium hydroxide in ALUDROX reacts with hydrochloric acid in the stomach.

(c) the carbonate and the acid in baking powder react.

5 CORROSION TESTING

The body of this car is made from steel. Steel is a mixture of iron and carbon.

Steel rusts or corrodes. Whatever it's called, it's a big nuisance. A rusty car is ugly. It may also be dangerous.

But the money may have to be spent. Replacing corroded objects like cars, bikes and bridges may be even more expensive!

The pictures show what happened to pieces of steel which were tested under different conditions.

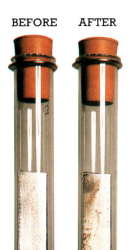

Oxygen gas only

Boiled water and nitrogen gas

Boiled water and oxygen gas

Nitrogen gas only

1. Copy out this table

	Water present?	Oxygen present?	Did the steel corrode?
A			
B			
C			
D			

2. Study the pictures and complete the table using ticks (√) or crosses (×).

3. Can steel corrode if oxygen is not present? Explain why you gave your answer.

4. Explain why the chemical name for rust is iron oxide.

5. What else must be present if steel is to corrode?

6. Explain why the grease on a bicycle chain stops the chain from corroding.

7. Describe what will happen if the paint on a car is chipped off and the steel below is exposed.

Steel corrodes more quickly in some places than in others. It is important to know why this is. Does the temperature or the amount of rainfall or pollution in the air make a difference? Answers to these questions will influence the decision of how much money to spend on corrosion protection.

It is also useful to know if steels with different compositions corrode at different speeds.

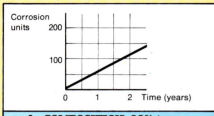

A: COMPOSITION: 98% iron
  2% carbon
WATER PRESENT: distilled
TEMPERATURE: 30°C

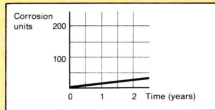

B: COMPOSITION: 97% iron
  2% carbon 1% chromium
WATER PRESENT: distilled
TEMPERATURE: 20°C

These results sheets are for tests like the ones shown in the pictures.

The conditions under which the tests were carried out have been recorded.

The graphs show the speed of corrosion over a period of two years. The steeper the slope, the faster the corrosion.

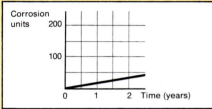

C: COMPOSITION: 98% iron
  2% carbon
WATER PRESENT: distilled
TEMPERATURE: 20°C

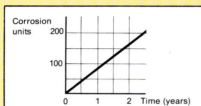

D: COMPOSITION: 98% iron
  2% carbon
WATER PRESENT: acidic/pH4
TEMPERATURE: 20°C

8. Use the results to find the effect of the following on the speed of corrosion.

   • increasing the temperature

   • the presence of acidic gases in the water

   • the presence of salt in the water

   • increasing the amount of chromium in the steel

   For each one, explain how you reached your conclusion.

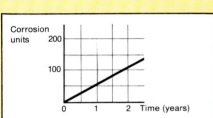

E: COMPOSITION: 97% iron
  1% chromium 2% carbon
WATER PRESENT: acidic/pH4
TEMPERATURE: 20°C

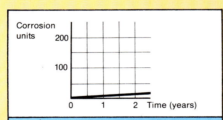

F: COMPOSITION: 93% iron
  5% chromium 2% carbon
WATER PRESENT: acidic/pH4
TEMPERATURE: 20°C

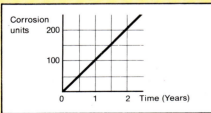

G: COMPOSITION: 98% iron
  2% carbon
WATER PRESENT: salty
TEMPERATURE: 20°C

9. Suggest TWO ways in which rainwater could become contaminated with salt.

10. Name TWO acidic gases which dissolve in rainwater.

11. Suggest a place in the United Kingdom where steel objects will corrode slowly. Explain your answer.

12. Copper is a metal which does not corrode. But a lot more iron than copper is used for making things. Suggest TWO reasons which might explain this.

6 ACCIDENT!

About 40 million tonnes of chemicals are carried each year on the roads of Britain.

Accidents sometimes happen. The lorry driver and emergency services must be ready to deal with any problems.

Each lorry carries emergency cards which tell people what to do in an accident.

Read the transport emergency card before answering these questions.

1. According to the card, the cargo is "Liquefied pressure gas with pungent odour".
   (a) How has the gas been liquefied (made liquid)?
   (b) What do you think is the reason why the gas is transported in liquid form?
   (c) Why is there a serious danger if the tanker gets hot?
   (d) What does "pungent odour" mean?

2. What are the main dangers of ammonia?

3. How could you protect yourself against ammonia?

4. A tanker carrying ammonia has crashed on the motorway. Two cars are also involved in the pile-up. Imagine you are in charge of the team sent to deal with the accident. Write an account of 100–150 words explaining what you would do.

Below is the emergency card for ammonia. The boiling point of ammonia is $-33°C$, so that at normal temperature and pressure it is a gas.

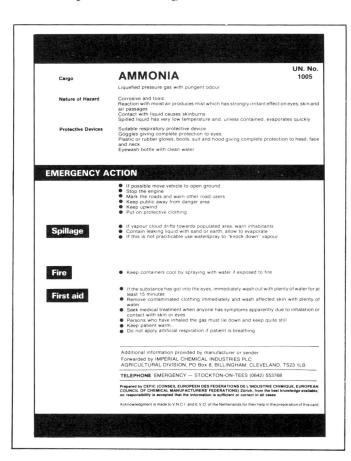

On the back of the crashed tanker in the photo, you will see that it has a large sign. This is the Hazchem sign. It contains simple codes which tell the emergency services what to do.

The Hazchem sign for ammonia is this:

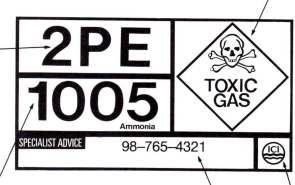

One of 13 special warning signs. This one says that ammonia is toxic, which means poisonous.

Code number for ammonia. Each chemical has its own number.

Name of the chemical company.

Emergency phone number for information.

The main code
The *number* shows which fire-fighting method should be used. In this case, fog (or spray) equipment is recommended.

The first *letter* gives more information. Look at the Hazchem scale below. Next to the P is a V, showing that ammonia is Very reactive. The scale also says that workers should wear *full* body protection (not just breathing apparatus) and the substance should be *diluted* with water.

Codes W, X, Y or Z are used to show that the substance must be *contained* (stopped from entering drains). Lastly, the E shows that emergency services should consider evacuating members of the public.

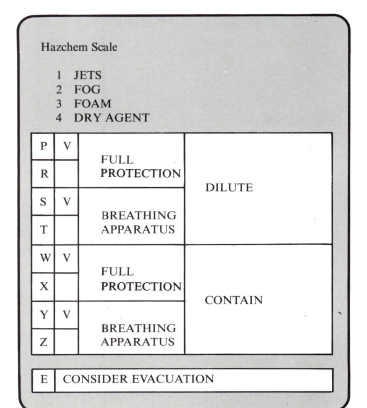

Hazchem Scale

1 JETS
2 FOG
3 FOAM
4 DRY AGENT

P	V	FULL PROTECTION	DILUTE
R			
S	V	BREATHING APPARATUS	
T			
W	V	FULL PROTECTION	CONTAIN
X			
Y	V	BREATHING APPARATUS	
Z			
E	CONSIDER EVACUATION		

5. Look at the crashed tanker in the photo.

   (a) What does the special warning sign immediately tell you about hydrochloric acid?

   (b) Which method should the fire brigade use on a spillage?

   (c) Should fire-fighters use full apparatus or breathing apparatus?

   (d) Should the acid be washed down drains?

6. Below is the Hazchem sign for petroleum fuel. What would you order fire-fighters to do if a petroleum fuel lorry crashed and caught fire?

7
SWAP SHOP

SWAP is a waste recycling project. It is Britain's largest voluntary project. In Leeds there are over one hundred collection points called "SWAP sites" where people can leave their waste for recycling. Paper, cans, bottles, clothing, aluminium and engine oil are all collected and then transferred to a processing plant.

> Save Waste And Prosper — SWAP

1. Name three articles made from aluminium that people might take to a SWAP site.

2. The five stages in the SWAP recycling scheme are given on the right. Arrange them in the order in which they take place.

   (a) delivering the processed waste to the re-user
   (b) delivering the waste to a processing plant
   (c) collecting the waste
   (d) re-using the processed waste
   (e) processing the waste

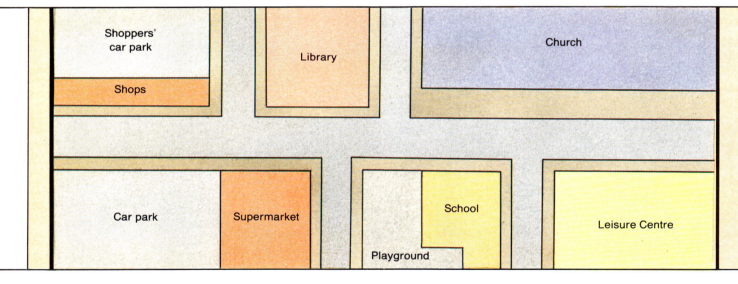

3. Melton is a suburb of Leeds. Look at the map of Melton. Use this map to choose *two* places where you might put a SWAP site.

   Explain your choices.

   Write down three questions you would want answered about each of these sites before choosing between them.

4. Leeds City Council want even more people to use the SWAP sites. They decide to hold a competition. To enter you have to complete the following sentence in not more than 10 words. "SWAP makes sense because…". What would your entry be?

WHY RECYCLE?

CREATES JOBS — PROTECTS THE ENVIRONMENT — CONSERVES RESOURCES — WASTE DISPOSAL COSTS ARE CUT — SAVES ENERGY

HOW TO RECYCLE

"Use the waste as a raw material for the same sort of product—waste paper for example."

"Re-use an object as it is—like milk bottles."

"Use the waste as a raw material for a different product—such as making compost."

"Burn the waste to get energy—incinerators can be used to heat buildings."

5. Use glass as an example to explain how recycling saves energy.

6. What is meant by "conserving resources"?

7. Give two examples of how recycling can protect the environment.

8. Someone argues that recycling means fewer jobs not more. Why might they think this?

9. Sort the contents of the dustbin into sets according to the uses they could be put to.

NOW YOU SEE IT . . . . . . NOW YOU DON'T

The SOLVENT is the liquid that does the DISSOLVING. The solvent in this bottle is water.

A solute and a solvent together make a SOLUTION—a liquid with something dissolved in it.

When insoluble stuff is mixed with a liquid it makes a SUSPENSION.

The sugar, colour and flavour from the lemons are all solutes. A SOLUTE is stuff that gets dissolved. Stuff that can dissolve is said to be SOLUBLE.

Things that do not dissolve like this flesh from the lemons are said to be INSOLUBLE.

1. Complete these sentences using the seven emphasised words above.
   You can only use each word *once*.

Sugar is _____ in tea. When made, the cup of tea is a _____ of sugar in tea.

Cola has carbon dioxide dissolved in it. The carbon dioxide is the _____ and water is the solvent.

The indigestion mixture is a _____. The medicine is _____ in the water in the bottle.

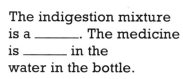

The white spirit is a _____. The paint is _____ in it.

2. Give one other everyday example of:

   (a) a solution made by dissolving a solid in a liquid.

   (b) a suspension.

   (c) a solution made by dissolving one liquid in another liquid.

16

Alan predicted that sugar cubes dissolve faster in hot water than in cold.

Here are Alan's results.

Temperature of water (°C)	30	45	50	65	70	85
Time to dissolve (seconds)	55	46	35	33	30	21

3. Describe four things that Alan should do to make his experiment a fair test.

4. Draw a point graph of Alan's results using axes like these:

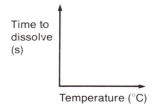

Use your graph to:

(a) complete this pattern; "the _____ the water, the _____ the sugar takes to dissolve."

(b) find the result which shows that Alan may have made a mistake. Explain your answer.

(c) predict how long the sugar would have taken to dissolve at 80°C.

(d) suggest what the temperature of the water was when the sugar cube took 49 seconds to dissolve.

5. (a) This diagram shows how the particles in a liquid are behaving. What happens to these particles as the water gets hotter?

(b) This diagram shows the dissolving taking place. Use this diagram and your previous answer to help you explain your answer to 4(a).

● Water particles   ○ Sugar particles

9 THE WATER CYCLE

Before you answer the questions, you should go round the Water Cycle. Start at the sea and follow the route that the water travels. Go down some of the different branches.

1. Where does the water evaporate?

2. Where does the water condense?

3. Explain why we can say that there is a "water cycle".

4. Copy out this table.

Place	What gets added to the water
In the water	Dissolved rock

The first entry in the table has been done for you. Find FOUR more places where things get added to water. Write them into the table.

5. "Pollution happens when things get added to the environment because of the activities of people." Give two examples of things being added to water that make it polluted. Give one example of something being added to water that is NOT pollution.

6. If you were a fish, you would know that oxygen dissolves in water. Suggest ONE place where oxygen is added to water. Why is it important for fish?

7. Chlorine is a germicide. Why is it added to tap water?

8. In some countries, drinking water is not chlorinated. Why should you drink "bottled" water when travelling in these countries?

9. Copy out this table.

Place	What gets separated from the water
Where the water rises from the sea	Salt in the sea water

The first entry has been done for you. Find TWO more places where things get separated from water. Write them into the table.

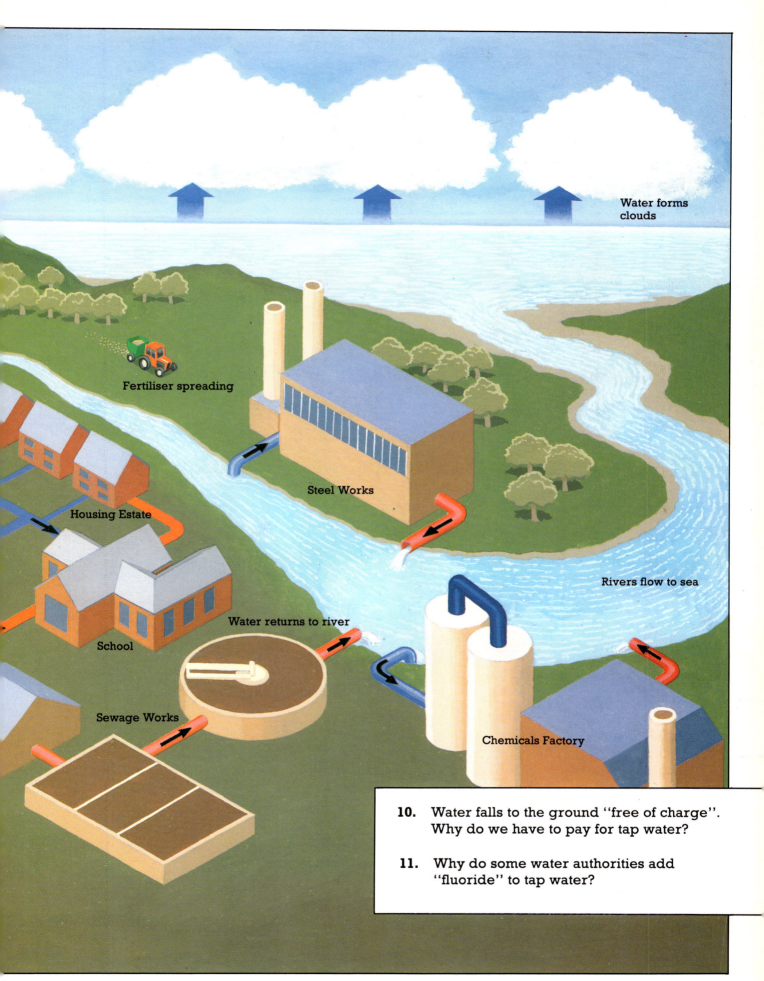

10. Water falls to the ground "free of charge". Why do we have to pay for tap water?

11. Why do some water authorities add "fluoride" to tap water?

10 ACID DROPS

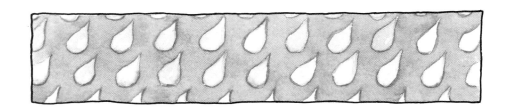

Sue and Ian are talking about their project on acid rain...

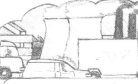

"Look, Sue, I didn't quite get what Mr Green said about acid rain"

"Well, he said we could find out the pH value of the rain each week"

"Oh yes, and pH 7 would be neutral like distilled water, wouldn't it?"

"Yes, a higher number means it's alkaline and a lower number means it's acidic. The scale goes from 0 to 14."

"And the lower the number the more acidic, right?"

"Yes, In fact, ordinary rain has a pH of 5.6."

"I remember now. It's slightly acidic because carbon dioxide dissolves in it."

"I expect our rain will often be more acidic because polluting gases like sulphur dioxide and nitrogen oxides dissolve in it as well."

"Those gases come from burning fossil fuels in power stations, industries and motor vehicles."

"That's why we're measuring wind direction as well as pH. I wonder if we'll be able to see where the acid rain comes from."

1. What is the pH of pure (distilled) water?

2. What is the pH of ordinary rain-water?

3. Why is ordinary rain-water acidic?

4. Which gases cause acid rain?

5. Where do the polluting gases come from?

6. What *two* important measurements are Sue and Ian going to make?

7. Where in your school would you set up a rain collector? Explain your decision.

Sue and Ian then set up their rain collector which looked like this:

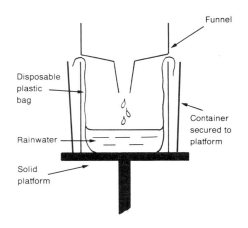

These were their instructions for using the rain collector:

(A) Use the pH indicator paper to measure the acidity. Avoid contaminating the rain-water with your fingers.

(B) Make a note of any visible contaminants like leaves, bird droppings or soot.

(C) Record the volume of water in cm³.

(D) Cover with a bag the hand that you use to remove the collecting bag. Then throw away the bag that was on your hand.

(E) Clean the funnel with distilled water, not tap water, and make sure it is dry.

(F) Make a summary of the weather conditions for the week.

8. Why did Sue and Ian look for "visible contaminants" like leaves?

9. Why did they have to change the collecting bag with another bag over their hand?

10. Why did the funnel have to be dried after washing out?

11. Why did they note the weather conditions?

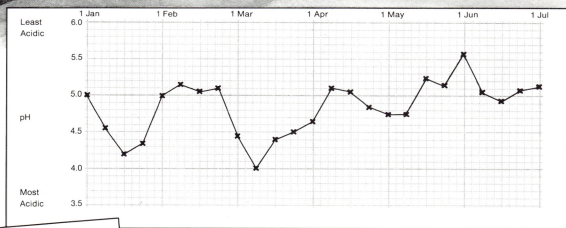

Main wind directions

Jan	1–14	SE
	15–31	SE
Feb	1–14	S
	15–28	SW
Mar	1–14	E
	15–31	NE
Apr	1–14	S
	15–30	SE
May	1–14	S
	15–31	SE
Jun	1–14	S
	15–30	SW

Over six months, Sue and Ian produced a graph of their pH readings and a table of the wind directions.

12. On what date was the pH value of the rain normal?

13. Around the middle of January the weather was very cold and more fuel was burnt than usual. Explain why the rain might have been more acidic at this time.

14. (a) During which month was the rain most acidic?
    (b) Look at the wind direction during that month. Suggest what might have caused the extra acidity.

11 FIRE!

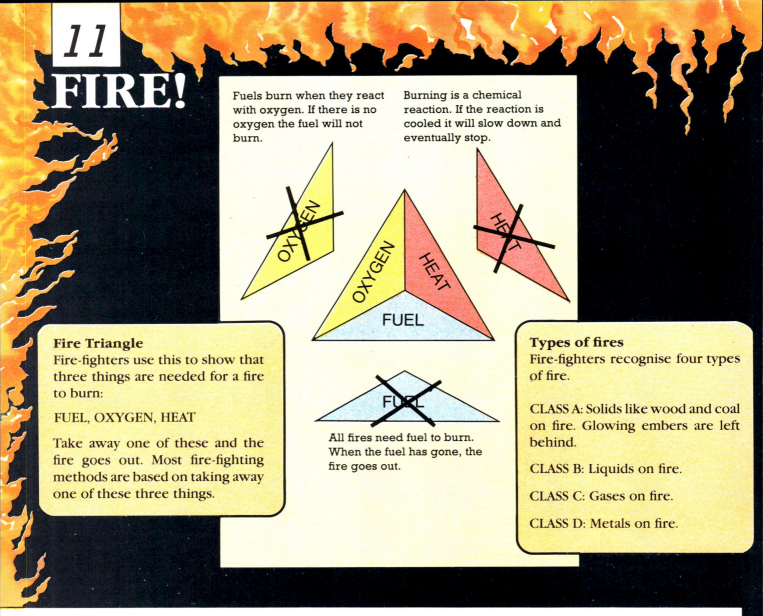

Fuels burn when they react with oxygen. If there is no oxygen the fuel will not burn.

Burning is a chemical reaction. If the reaction is cooled it will slow down and eventually stop.

Fire Triangle
Fire-fighters use this to show that three things are needed for a fire to burn:

FUEL, OXYGEN, HEAT

Take away one of these and the fire goes out. Most fire-fighting methods are based on taking away one of these three things.

All fires need fuel to burn. When the fuel has gone, the fire goes out.

Types of fires
Fire-fighters recognise four types of fire.

CLASS A: Solids like wood and coal on fire. Glowing embers are left behind.

CLASS B: Liquids on fire.

CLASS C: Gases on fire.

CLASS D: Metals on fire.

Many different ways of stopping or fighting fires are listed below.

For each one, *explain* which part of the fire triangle is being taken away.

1. Spraying water over a burning wooden building.
2. Putting a bread board over a chip pan which has caught fire.
3. Leaving gaps between the trees in large forests. These gaps are known as "fire-breaks".
4. Switching off the supply to a leaking gas main which is on fire.
5. Spraying carbon dioxide at a burning laboratory bench.
6. Closing all doors and windows when leaving during a fire alarm.
7. Covering burning rubbish with a fire-proof blanket.
8. Installing fire doors in a large hotel.

Water in action
Cools and smothers.
Especially used for Class A fires.

Dry powder in action
Puts out gas fires.
Difficult to use in confined spaces because it cuts down visibility.

Foam in action
Often used for oil fires.

Carbon dioxide
Smothers the fire.
Not good in open areas where it can be blown away.

Halon
These extinguishers contain special liquids which vapourise in the fire and stop the burning reaction. The fumes are poisonous but, like carbon dioxide, they can be blown away.

9. What class of fire is each of the following?

   (a) Wood fire   (b) Hull of a ship on fire

   (c) Burning gas main (d) Chip pan fire

10. Suggest why Class A fires are more difficult to extinguish outdoors.

11. Which types of extinguisher on this page would leave little mess?

12. Suggest why water rather than dry powder extinguishers are usually put in busy public buildings.

13. Water reacts with many hot metals to make hydrogen gas. Why might water make Class D fires *more* dangerous and not put them out?

14. Why is water not the best substance to use to put out an electrical fire?

15. Why might it be dangerous to use a Halon extinguisher in a confined space?

12
GETTING BREAD TO RISE

In the Middle East, the most common everyday bread is called khubz. It is becoming very popular in this country where it is known as pitta bread.

The recipe for khubz (pitta bread) and a recipe for a traditional British loaf are given below.

KHUBZ (PITTA BREAD)
Mix wholemeal flour with white flour and add enough water to make a dough. Flatten small lumps of the dough and heat under a hot grill for 2 minutes on each side.

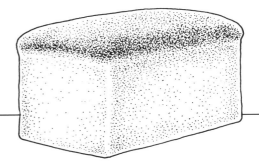

WHITE BREAD
Mix salt and flour together in a bowl. Then add a mixture of yeast, sugar and warm water to make a dough. Leave the dough in a warm place for one hour. Bake in a hot oven (225 °C) for one hour.

1. Copy out and complete the following table to show the differences between the two types of bread.

	Khubz	White bread
What it looks like		
Ingredients		
How it is baked		

The important extra ingredient in the white bread is yeast. Yeast is a fungus. It changes the sugars present in the mixture, to form ethanol and carbon dioxide gas. This process is called **fermentation**.

It is the carbon dioxide which is released during this fermentation that makes the white bread rise. The yeast is called a "raising agent".

This graph shows the change in the size of a piece of dough from the time that it is made to the time that it is completely baked.

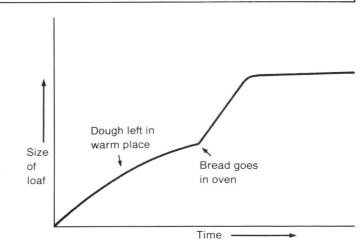

2. Copy out the table. Match up the statements given opposite with the correct stage in the breadmaking process.

Stage in the process	What is happening
(a) The dough is rising slowly	
(b) The dough is in the oven and is rising quickly	
(c) The dough has stopped rising	

- The yeast has been killed by the heat from the oven.

- The rate of fermentation is increased by the effect of the heat from the oven.

- Yeast begins to ferment the sugar in bread. Carbon dioxide gas forms.

- The carbon dioxide gas in the dough expands as it gets hot.

3. Ethanol is a liquid which has a low boiling point. What will happen to the ethanol produced by the fermentation when the bread is baked?

Bakestone bread is still baked in Wales.

BAKESTONE BREAD
Mix flour, salt and water in a bowl. Dissolve a teaspoon full of bicarbonate of soda in a little milk and add to the mixture. Bake the dough in a moderate oven (200°C) for 40 minutes.

The "raising agent" in this recipe is bicarbonate of soda. Its chemical name is sodium hydrogencarbonate.

When it is heated, it forms carbon dioxide gas, water and sodium carbonate. Sodium carbonate has an unpleasant taste.

Here is a recipe for scones.

PLAIN SCONES
Mix together some flour, salt and lard. Add 2 teaspoon measures of bicarbonate of soda and 4 teaspoon measures of cream of tartar. Bake in an oven at 225°C for 10 minutes.

The chemical names for the two "raising agents" are sodium hydrogencarbonate and tartaric acid. When these chemicals get wet, they react together to form carbon dioxide gas.

4. Complete this word equation to show what happens during the baking.

sodium hydrogencarbonate → ___ + ___ + ___

5. This type of chemical reaction is called "thermal decomposition". Why "thermal" and why "decomposition"?

6. Why do you think that sodium hydrogencarbonate on its own is not commonly used as a raising agent for bread?

7. Explain why the reaction which takes place is an example of neutralisation.

8. Why do you think it important to get the ingredients present in the right amounts?

9. Some baking powders contain sodium hydrogencarbonate and tartaric acid ready mixed. Why do these baking powders have to be stored in a dry place?

13 SALT OF THE EARTH

People who live and travel in very hot countries may sweat a lot. They have to eat extra salt to replace what is lost in their sweat. If they don't have enough salt, they get cramp.

In parts of Tanzania the soil contains a lot of salt. The woman shown in this picture knows how to separate salt from the mud. The equipment she is using is a good example of "appropriate technology".

She is using shells from a tree fruit for containers. They are called gourds. The one she is pouring a liquid into has holes at both ends. She has put a layer of thin leaves at the bottom of this gourd.

In the picture below, she is using a wood fire to heat salt solution in the open tray.

1. Draw a line diagram to show the inside of the gourds. Show the holes and the leaves.

2. Write a description of how you think the people in Tanzania get salt crystals from the mud.

   You must use these words in your description: dissolve, solution, filter, evaporate, crystallise.

3. Look again at the equipment the woman is using. What do you think is meant by "appropriate technology"?

SALT OF THE SEA

On the coast of Tanzania, salt is extracted from sea water. Tanzanian engineers have built a salt works to separate salt from the other chemicals in sea water.

The engineers began by finding out about the solubility of different chemicals in sea water. This table shows the maximum amount of three different chemicals that will dissolve in 1 litre of water.

Chemical	Number of grams that can be dissolved in 1 litre water at 20 °C
Sodium chloride	360
Magnesium chloride	544
Calcium sulphate	2.4

4. Which of the chemicals in the table is
   (a) the most soluble in water?
   (b) the least soluble in water?

5. Explain why the Tanzanian engineers predicted that when sea water is evaporated, the first crystals to form are calcium sulphate.

Sodium chloride is the chemical name for salt.

From this information the engineers could tell what would happen when sea water is evaporated. They predicted that the first crystals to form would be calcium sulphate.

The diagram opposite shows what happens at the salt works near Dar-es-Salaam.

Sea water is pumped into a large shallow pond. Some of the water evaporates. Calcium sulphate crystallises out.

The concentrated sea water is then pumped into another pond. More water evaporates. Salt (sodium chloride) crystallises out.

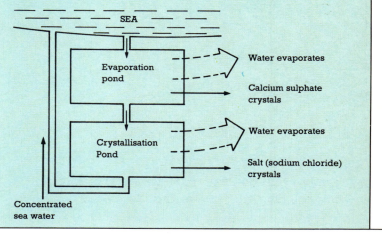

6. What is the source of energy used for evaporating the water?

7. Suggest why it is important to remove the calcium sulphate from sea water before the salt crystallises out.

8. Not all the water is allowed to evaporate from the second pond. The water that is left is pumped back into the sea. What impurity does this water contain? Explain your answer.

9. Why do you think this method of extracting salt from sea water is not used in Britain?

14 ALCOOL

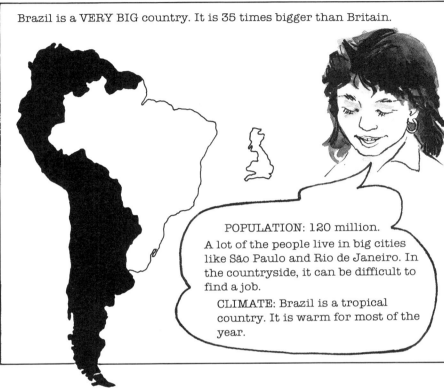

Brazil is a VERY BIG country. It is 35 times bigger than Britain.

POPULATION: 120 million.
A lot of the people live in big cities like São Paulo and Rio de Janeiro. In the countryside, it can be difficult to find a job.

CLIMATE: Brazil is a tropical country. It is warm for most of the year.

Your Task

Write a newspaper article for the "Daily Globe".

Design your page like a newspaper. The headline has been done for you.

In your article, you must include the following:
- why there was a problem,
- the scientists' solution to the problem,
- the benefits for the people of Brazil.

KEY IDEAS: high price of crude oil, renewable resources, fermentation, employment, distillation, pollution problems.

BUY YOUR "LEAD FREE" ALCOOL HERE. IT IS VERY GOOD SENHORA!

In 1975, the Brazilian government began to worry about the rising cost of crude oil. Most of the oil had to be bought from other countries. Petrol for cars was becoming very expensive.

"WE CAN'T GO ON PAYING LIKE THIS — IF ONLY THERE WAS AN ALTERNATIVE SOURCE OF FUEL FOR CARS"

SOLAR POWER? TOO SPREAD OUT!

COAL? DO WE REALLY WANT STEAM DRIVEN CARS?

NUCLEAR? PEOPLE WOULDN'T DRIVE NUCLEAR CARS!

PLANTS? NOW THERE'S A THOUGHT...

Plants "lock up" the sun's energy in the food they make during photosynthesis. How could this stored energy be used?

Brazilian scientists said that sugar cane could provide the answer.

There is a lot of space in Brazil for growing this plant. It grows well in warm countries.

A new crop of sugar cane can be grown every year—it is a renewable resource.

400 new sugar cane plantations have been built.

A fermentation tank for producing alcohol

Sugar cane plant

A Brazilian sugar plantation

This factory turns sugar cane into alcohol by a process called fermentation.

Alcohol can be used in cars instead of petrol. Brazilians call it ALCOOL.

Because alcohol has a boiling point of 79°C, it can be separated from water by distillation.

2 million jobs have been created. Lead pollution in the city of São Paulo has been reduced.

Only the oil sellers are disappointed. They have lost 9 million dollars a year.

15 CAMPING GAS

Many people spend part of their holidays camping or carvanning. They need to take a cooking stove with them. There are many different types of camping stoves. Some use petrol, others use paraffin or wood. The most popular stoves for camping use gas.

1. What name is given to substances like paraffin, petrol, wood and gas which can be used as a source of heat?

2. Suggest why each of the following is not as popular as gas for camping stoves. Give a different reason for each one.
   (a) wood
   (b) petrol
   (c) paraffin

Here are some safety rules for using gas stoves.

- Check for leaks using soapy water.
- NEVER check for leaks with a naked flame.
- Make sure there is a lot of fresh air getting to the burner.
- Do not sleep in a room where gas cylinders are stored.

3. Explain how soapy water could be used to check for gas leaks.

4. Why should you never check for gas leaks with a naked flame?

5. Why should you allow a lot of air to get to a gas stove?

6. Why should cylinders of gas not be stored in your tent or caravan?

This information is from the book *Camping and Caravanning in Europe* (published by AA).

FUELS
"The gases in the cans and cylinder are mainly butane or propane. Both of these gases are kept as liquids by pressurising them. When the tap on the gas stove is opened, the pressure is reduced. This allows the liquid to turn into a gas. Propane and butane are both widely available in Europe. Propane is more likely to be used in cold countries."

7. Copy out the table. Use information from the diagram on the right to help you to complete it.

Temperature (°C)	Propane	Butane
20	gas	
−20		liquid
−50		

(i) 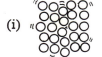 (ii)   (iii) O O O

8. Which of the diagrams (i), (ii) or (iii) best represents the arrangement of butane particles at (a) 20 °C and (b) −20 °C?

9. Describe the difference between the arrangement and movement of the particles in a liquid and in a gas.

10. Why does increasing the pressure help to turn gases to liquids?

11. Why is it easier to carry propane and butane as liquids rather than gases?

12. What happens to the liquids in the canisters when the gas tap is opened?

13. In many cold countries, the temperature often falls below −20 °C. Explain the problem of using butane gas in camping stoves in cold countries.

14. Methane gas boils at −164 °C. It is used a lot in our homes. Why do you think it is not used in camping stoves?

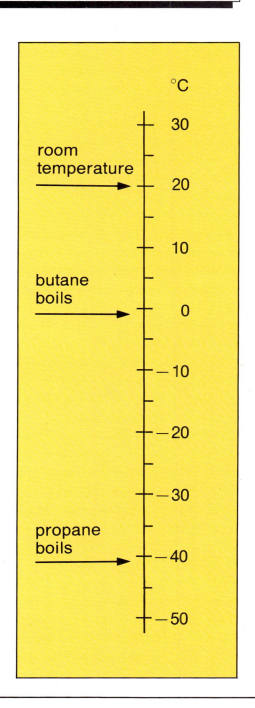

31

16 FIZZY DRINKS

Many fizzy drinks are made by dissolving carbon dioxide gas in water. The label on the bottle tells you that you are drinking "carbonated water".

Carbon dioxide makes water slightly acidic. This is why fizzy drinks have a sharp taste.

This table shows you the volume of carbon dioxide that can be dissolved in a litre bottle of water at different temperatures. It also shows you the pH of the solution you get.

Temperature	0°C	10°C	20°C
Volume of carbon dioxide (cm^3)	1700	1200	900
pH	3.0	3.5	4.0

1. What volume of carbon dioxide gas do you think can be dissolved in a litre bottle of water at 15°C?

2. What happens to the solubility of carbon dioxide in water as the temperature rises?

3. On a hot day, the pressure inside a bottle of fizzy pop increases. The bottle could even explode. Explain why this happens.

Some pop bottles are made of plastic.

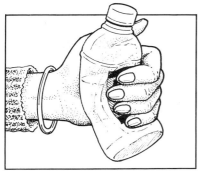

This bottle is half full of water. It is easy to squash.

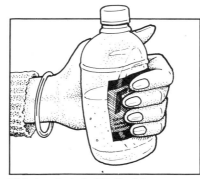

This bottle is half full of fizzy pop. It is difficult to squash.

4. Why do you think it is hard to squash a bottle which has fizzy pop in it?

5. Give TWO advantages of using plastic instead of glass for pop bottles.

6. Give ONE disadvantage of using plastic for pop bottles.

7. What would you do to find the pH of fizzy drinks?

8. What happens to the pH of water when more carbon dioxide is dissolved in it?

9. If you want to stop fizzy drinks going flat you should

   - keep the top on the bottle
   - keep the bottle in a cold place

   Explain how these two things stop fizzy drinks going flat.

Some fizzy drinks come in cans like this one from America. The cans are made from aluminium. The inside of the can is coated with a very thin layer of plastic. Aluminium is an expensive metal to produce.

10. Why do you think that the aluminium has to be coated with plastic? (HINT: acids)

11. What TWO things have the makers of COLA FIZZ done to encourage people to return the can so that the metal can be used again?

LIVER SALTS and ALKA TABS relieve indigestion. When the powder or the tablets are put into water, some of the ingredients react together and make carbon dioxide gas.

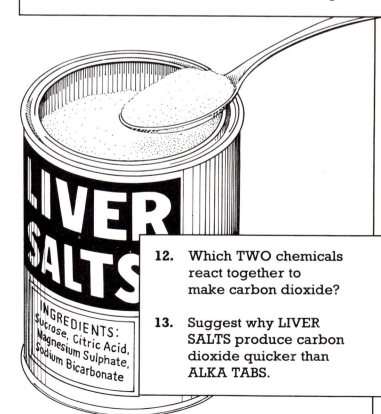

12. Which TWO chemicals react together to make carbon dioxide?

13. Suggest why LIVER SALTS produce carbon dioxide quicker than ALKA TABS.

17
FEED THE WORLD

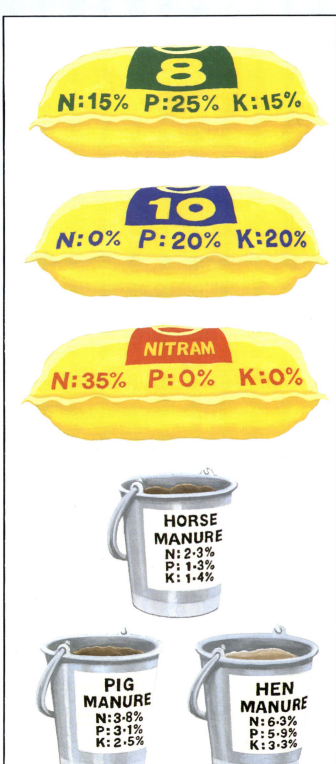

Plants need nitrogen, phosphorus and potassium if they are to grow healthily. Fertilisers are chemicals which contain these plant nutrients. Natural fertilisers like manure are still being used, but most of the fertilisers that are used today are made by chemical companies. Different fertilisers contain different percentages of important plant nutrients.

1. Which artificial fertiliser contains most nitrogen?

2. Which natural fertiliser contains least potassium?

3. Which artificial fertiliser would you choose if you wanted to feed your crops nitrogen, phosphorus and potassium?

4. Which natural fertiliser contains the greatest percentage of the three nutrients?

5. Why do farmers not make greater use of the fertiliser you have named in Question 4?

6. "Straight" fertilisers only contain *one* of the nutrients that plants need. Which of these fertilisers is a straight fertiliser?

7. The diagrams below show what happens to one type of plant if it does not get enough of these nutrients. Which fertiliser would you use on a field where:

   (a) the crops had weak roots?
   (b) the crops had small thin leaves?

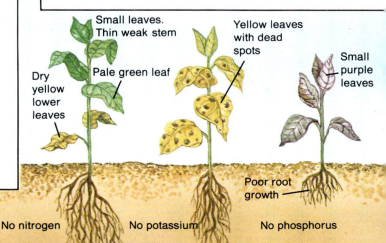

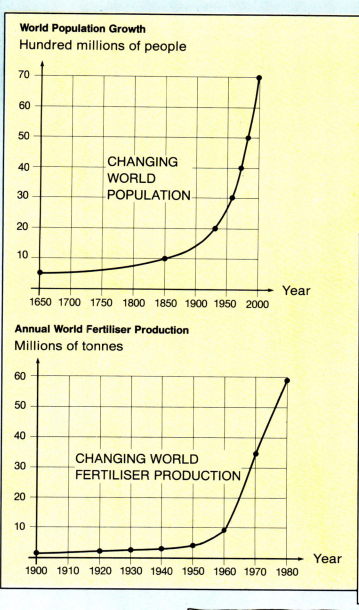

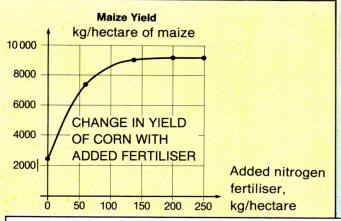

8. These graphs will help you to understand how fertilisers help "to feed the world". Complete this passage:

"It took ____ years from 1650 to ____ for the world population to double. It only took ____ years from ____ to 1930 for it to double again. To help feed the growing number of people, farmers are using more and more fertiliser. From 1920 to ____ the world production of fertiliser increased from ____ to 59 millions of tonnes per year. Adding 100kg of nitrogen fertiliser per hectare to a field means ____ kg of maize can be harvested. If more than ____ kg of fertiliser are added, however, no further improvement is gained."

9. Different people say different things about our increasing use of fertilisers. Decide what you think, and write a paragraph of about 100 words explaining your views.

"Fertilisers are a main cause of nitrate pollution in water supplies."

"Fertilisers reduce the cost of food."

"High levels of nitrates in rivers and streams can lead to the death of fish."

"We waste $\frac{2}{3}$ of our animal manure."

"Nitrates have always been present in soil, water, plants and people."

"Fertiliser use is vital for increased food production."

"Bags of fertiliser are as important as bags of wheat for developing countries."

"Fertilisers are expensive because a lot of energy is used to make them."

"Without fertilisers we would not be able to feed the world's population."

"High nitrate levels in drinking water may cause cancer in adults and oxygen deficiency in young babies. Some experts disagree with this."

"Animal manure does not provide an instant supply of nitrates."

"It takes several years before nitrates in fertilisers reach water supplies."

18

OIL INDUSTRIES PLC

Internal Memo
To: Chief Chemist
From: Refinery Manager
Date: 1 December

Cassie

I enclose four chemicals separated by distilling crude oil at our refinery. We have decided to move into the lubricating oil market and we need to know which of these chemicals would be the best to market as an engine oil. Please let me have your team's report on this as soon as possible.

What sort of properties do you think an engine oil should have, Steve?

Well, for a start it should NOT be corrosive.

Yes, and it should be runny so that it can get to all the parts of the engine where it's needed.

None of these chemicals are corrosive and I have an idea how we can test them for runniness. Here, look at this diagram.

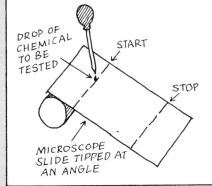

We'll have to be careful to make it a fair test, but let's give it a try.

SOME TIME LATER

I'll start with chemical B. Ready with the stopclock. Go.

That one took $11\frac{1}{2}$ seconds. Try chemical C next.

1. What does the word "corrosive" mean?

2. What process is used to separate the chemicals in an oil refinery?

3. Why did Cassie say that the engine oil should be runny?

4. State three things that Cassie and Steve did to make the comparison of the chemicals fair.

5. Draw a table to show Cassie's and Steve's results.

WHICH OIL?

OK. here goes.

C took 12 seconds.

I'm putting chemical A on the slide now. Start the stopclock.

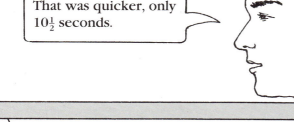

That was quicker, only $10\frac{1}{2}$ seconds.

Now for the last one—chemical D.

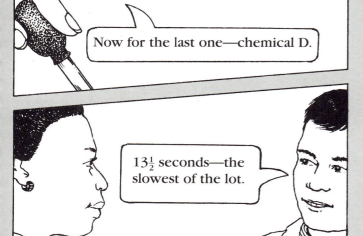

$13\frac{1}{2}$ seconds—the slowest of the lot.

6. From their results, which chemical would you choose as the best engine oil? Give a reason for your answer.

7. While doing some research in the company library, Cassie found out this information about the molecules in A, B, C and D.

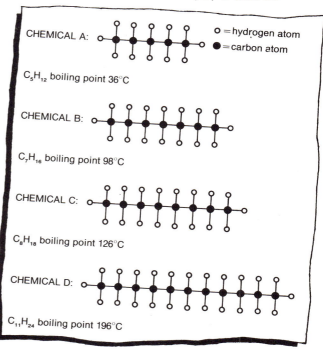

CHEMICAL A: ○ = hydrogen atom ● = carbon atom
C_5H_{12} boiling point 36°C

CHEMICAL B:
C_7H_{16} boiling point 98°C

CHEMICAL C:
C_8H_{18} boiling point 126°C

CHEMICAL D:
$C_{11}H_{24}$ boiling point 196°C

How does this information help you to understand how these chemicals can be separated by fractional distillation?

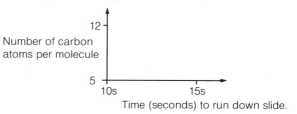

8. Using axes and scales like the ones above, plot a graph of the time taken to run down the slide against the number of carbon atoms per molecule.

9. Use your graph to

   (a) state the pattern shown by these results.
   (b) work out the times that it would take chemicals with 6 and 12 carbon atoms per molecule to run down the slide.

10. Suggest an explanation for the pattern you have stated.

11. When an engine is running, the oil will warm up to 100°C. Which chemical do you think would make the best engine oil NOW? Explain your answer.

19 HEALTHY EATING

In 1970, a survey was carried out to find out how many men between the ages of 45 and 54 died of heart disease. The scientists compared samples of 100 000 men in 17 different countries. They also found out the percentage of the energy in a typical diet that comes from eating fat.

	Deaths per 100 000 men	% of total energy from fat
Finland	403	48
USA	346	51
Scotland	343	47
Australia	297	52
New Zealand	273	37
Canada	270	41
England and Wales	259	45
Norway	213	41
Czechoslovakia	201	36
Germany	194	30
Israel	148	31
Bulgaria	72	31
France	66	29
Romania	61	27
Spain	50	31
Hong Kong	34	26
Japan	34	28

The figures show that the more fat you eat, the more likely you are to die of heart disease

DR SMITH

This shows that there is *no* link between fat in men's diet and heart disease.

DR JONES

This shows that there is a strong link between fat in men's diet and death from heart disease, but other things play a part as well.

DR PATEL

1. (a) Arrange in order the four countries where fat in the diet gives men the most energy.

   (b) Arrange in order the four countries where fat in the diet gives men the least energy.

2. Do the same thing for the four countries which have (a) the highest (b) the lowest death rate from heart disease amongst men aged 45–54.

3. Which expert do you agree with: Dr Smith, Dr Patel or Dr Jones? Use your lists from Questions 1 and 2 to help you explain your answer.

Experts have looked into the links between diet and health. Their general advice was:

"Eat less fat, salt and sugar. Eat more fibre"

4. Design a poster to illustrate this advice. Try to make your poster simple, visual and easy to understand.

BRAN FLAKES

CEREAL ONLY WITHOUT MILK OR SUGAR

AVERAGE COMPOSITION	PER 30g (1oz) serving	PER 100g (3½oz)
Energy	444kJ/106kcal	1482kJ/354kcal
Fat	0.3g	1.0g
Protein	2.6g	8.0g
Carbohydrate	25.0g	84.0g
Dietary Fibre	3.3g	11.0g
Added Salt	0.9g	3.1g
Added Sugar (Sucrose)	2.0g	6.5g
MINERALS/VITAMINS	PERCENTAGE OF THE RECOMMENDED DAILY AMOUNT	
Thiamin (B_1)	30%	1.2mg
Riboflavin (B_2)	30%	1.6mg
Niacin	30%	18.0mg
Folic Acid	30%	300.0µg
Vitamin B_{12}	30%	2.0µg
Vitamin D_3	30%	2.5µg
Iron	17%	6.7mg

THIS PACK CONTAINS APPROXIMATELY 12 SERVINGS

Tesco Stores are putting nutrition information onto the labels of their brand foods to help their customers choose healthy foods.

This nutrition information is given in two ways, and these are shown here.

 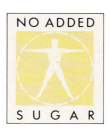 

5. Suggest one *advantage* and one *disadvantage* of each of these two ways of showing nutrition information?

Use the information on the cereal packet to answer the next question.

6. (a) What are the two units used to measure the energy in the cereal?

(b) What do the symbols g, mg and µg stand for?

(c) Which mineral or vitamin is present in the largest amount in 100g of the cereal?

(d) Which mineral or vitamin is present in the *smallest* amount in 100g of the cereal?

(e) For which mineral or vitamin does a 30g serving contribute *least* to the total amount needed in a day?

20 EXTRACTING ZINC

There are tiny amounts of zinc everywhere – in soil, seawater and rocks. Usually, the amounts are so small that it is not worth getting them out. There is a lot of zinc in a mineral called sphalerite. But ...

- sphalerite is found underground,
- it is mixed up with other bits of rock.

Only about $\frac{1}{5}$ of the rock that is dug out of the ground is sphalerite. The rest of the rock is waste.

Every year, about 5 million tonnes of zinc metal are produced throughout the world. Zinc is used to coat other metals and is also an important part of many mixtures of metals (alloys).

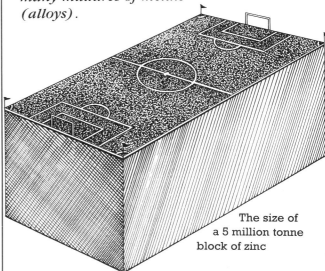

The size of a 5 million tonne block of zinc

The chemical name for sphalerite is zinc sulphide. It is a compound of zinc and sulphur.

It is difficult to extract zinc from zinc sulphide. The zinc sulphide is first heated with oxygen from the air. This changes the zinc sulphide into zinc oxide and the sulphur into sulphur dioxide gas. This gas is corrosive and so is not allowed to escape into the atmosphere. It is used to make sulphuric acid.

1. If a mining company digs out 100 000 tonnes of rock each year from a zinc mine, how much waste rock will there be?

2. The waste rock is dumped on tips. Why is this an environmental problem?

3. Suggest TWO things that could be done to reduce this problem.

4. Complete this word equation to show what happens.

    zinc sulphide + oxygen → ___ + ___

5. Why is sulphur dioxide not allowed to escape into the atmosphere?

6. Name the important acid that is made from the sulphur dioxide.

Now we've got the zinc oxide—what's next? There are two ways of extracting zinc from zinc oxide.

The Electrolytic Process
80% of zinc is produced by electrolysis.

The zinc oxide is first reacted with sulphuric acid to make a concentrated solution of zinc sulphate. The solution is poured into an electrolysis cell. The zinc sulphate solution is split up (decomposed) by the electricity passing through it. Zinc metal collects at the negative electrode. Oxygen gas is produced at the positive electrode.

7. Where do you think the sulphuric acid used in this part of the process comes from?

8. You cannot see the inside of the electrolysis cell in the picture. Copy out and label this cross-section through the electrolysis cell.

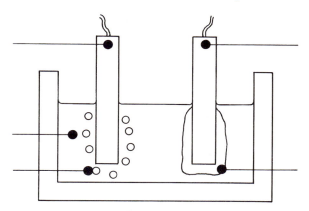

9. Copy out and complete this table for the electrolytic process.

What is used up	What is produced

The Thermal Process
About 20% of zinc is produced in a blast furnace.

Zinc oxide and coke (carbon) are poured into the top of the furnace. Hot air is pumped in through holes at the bottom.
The coke burns in the air to form a gas called carbon monoxide.
This gas then removes the oxygen from the zinc oxide to form zinc and carbon dioxide gas.
The furnace is very hot, and so the zinc forms a vapour. It is carried up to the top of the furnace where it is cooled and turns into a liquid.

10. You cannot see the inside of the furnace in the picture. Copy out and label this cross-section through the furnace.

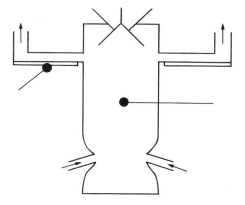

11. Copy out and complete this table for the thermal process.

What is used up	What is produced

Matrix of the Relationship between Activities and Attainment Targets of the National Curriculum

	1 Gold	2 Oil	3 Kitchen Cleaners	4 Acids	5 Corrosion Testing	6 Accident!	7 Swap Shop	8 Now you see it...	9 The Water Cycle	10 Acid Drops	11 Fire!	12 Getting Bread to Rise	13 Salt of the Earth	14 Alcool	15 Camping Gas	16 Fizzy Drinks	17 Feed the World	18 Which Oil?	19 Healthy Eating	20 Extracting Zinc
1 Exploration of science					✓												✓	✓		
2 The variety of life																✓				
5 Human influences on the Earth	✓						✓			✓									✓	
6 Types and uses of materials		✓	✓					✓	✓				✓	✓	✓					
7 Making new materials		✓		✓				✓	✓			✓	✓		✓		✓		✓	
8 Explaining how materials behave			✓						✓		✓			✓					✓	
9 Earth and Atmosphere						✓					✓									
13 Energy		✓																		

INDEX

Numbers refer to units, not pages.

acid rain   10
acids   4
alcohol fuel   14
alkalis   3, 4
ammonia   6

baking   12
bitumen   2
blast furnace   20
bleach   3
boiling points   15
butane gas   15

camping gas   15
carbonate   4
carbon dioxide   11, 12, 16
chlorine   9
condensation   9
corrosion   5, 18
crude oil   2, 14
crystallisation   13

detergent   3
diesel oil   2
dissolving   13
distillation   14

electrolysis   20
energy units   19
evaporation   9, 13

fat   19
fermentation   12, 14
fertilisers   17
filtration   9, 13
finite resources   2
fire extinguishers   11
fire fighting   11
fire triangle   11
fizzy drinks   16
fizzy sweets   4
fluoride   9
fractional distillation   2
fractions   2
fuel   11

gases, expansion of   12
gold   1

halon   11
Hazchem scale   6
heart disease   19
hydrocarbons   2
hydrochloric acid   6

indigestion tablets   4
irritant   3

kerosene   2
kitchen cleaners   3

lemon juice   4
limestone   3
lubricating oil   2

magnesium hydroxide   4
metal hydroxide   4
metallic properties   1
metal oxide   4
molecules   18

naphtha   2
nitrate levels in drinking water   17
nitrogen oxide   10
nutrition information   19

oven cleaner   3
oxygen   9

panning   1
particle model   8, 15
petroleum fuel   2, 6
photosynthesis   14
pH value   3, 5, 10, 16
pollution   9, 14
propane gas   15

raising agent   12
reaction rate   3, 5, 16
recycling   7, 16
renewable resources   14
rust   4, 5

safety   6
salt extraction   13
salts   4
scouring powder   3
sodium hydrogencarbonate   12
sodium hydroxide   3
solubility   13
solute   8
solution   8, 13
solvent   8
sphalerite   20
stainless steel   5
steel   5
sugar cane   14
sulphur dioxide   10, 20
suspension   8

tartaric acid   12
thermal decomposition   12

waste tips   20
water cycle   9

yeast   12

zinc extraction   20

43

Acknowledgements

The publishers would like to thank the following for supplying photographs for these units:

3 Jeyes Ltd (the *Parazone* label); Lever Industrial Ltd (the *Vim* label); Reckitt & Colman Products Ltd, the proprietors of the trade mark *Oven Pad*. All copyright in the pack copy remains with Reckitt & Colman Products Ltd.

4 Green's of Brighton (*Borwick's Baking Powder*); Permalite Ltd (*Jenolite*); Wyeth Laboratories (*Aludrox* tablets).

5 David Edwards (the test tube experiments); Sandra Wegerif (the rusting car).

6 ICI Chemicals and Polymers.

11 Chubb Ltd (the foam, carbon dioxide and halon extinguishers); The London Fire Brigade (fire fighting using water); The Offshore Fire Training Centre (the dry powder extinguisher—2 photographs).

13 David Morgan.

14 Wayland Publishers.

19 Tesco Stores.

20 The British Museum, Geological Museum (the zinc ore); Commonwealth Smelting Ltd (the blast furnace and the roasting plant of a zinc smelter); Lurgi AG, Frankfurt-am-Main and Mr K. N. Hewitt, Norzinc (UK) Ltd (the electrolysis cell).

Artwork for the following spreads was produced by:

Jane Cope 1, 3; Sean MacGarry 1, 2, 8, 9, 12, 15, 16, 17, 20; Juliet Snape 4, 7, 10, 11, 17, 18, 19; Margaret Theakson 14